THE
DATING COACH
WORKBOOK

Combining Therapy and Marketing for a Happy, Healthy and Successful Dating Life

Utilized in the Dating Coach Program at

RESOLUTIONS
RELATIONSHIPS FAMILY BUSINESS

www.resolutions-az.com

BECKY JOHNSTON, MA, MBA, CM, LPC

Copyright © 2012 Becky Johnston
All rights reserved.

ISBN: 1467916110
ISBN 13: 9781467916110

Becky Johnston, MA, MBA, CM, LPC
Founder, The Dating Coach Program

Becky Johnston is a practicing psychotherapist in the Phoenix Metropolitan Area. Her practice specializes in couples, families and teenagers, as well as divorce and small business mediation and counseling. She discovered a need over the years, while counseling couples. She discovered that, sadly, many people had not made very wise decisions with regard to their partner choice, and their compatibility with that partner was lacking. Many of these couples were simply too incompatible to salvage a satisfying relationship. This initial poor choice was due in part to individual therapeutic issues that needed to be resolved before entering the relationship. Once resolved, an individual will have much greater success finding a compatible partner, which will have much greater success resulting in a successful relationship. Becky also discovered that many people who were single were very uncomfortable dating or continued to have failed relationship after failed relationship because they were blindly entering the dating world without a plan. We have plans for home ownership, careers, parenting, but not for the most important relationship that we enter. And finally, Becky discovered that one's discomfort with dating often was the catalyst for entering a marriage that was destined to be incompatible. If you welcome dating, have more knowledge of self and others, overcome personal obstacles, execute a plan and measure results, your dating life is going to improve.

Becky spent 20 years prior to becoming a therapist and mediator working as a Marketing Executive. Thus the idea was created to approach dating from both a therapeutic and marketing standpoint in order to attract the best options possible, in order to ultimately lead to the happiest and most successful relationship possible.

Your mindset entering therapy with The Dating Coach

Unless you indicate otherwise, you are entering this program because you want something to change – you want better results from your dating and relationship life. This means that you may have to change something. You can't change who you are and would never ultimately be happy doing so, but you will have to change some actions, some thoughts, some approaches to dating and relationships. This may not always be comfortable. And you may have to give something up to gain success in this area of your life. It is required that you are open to change.

In addition, there are going to be times perhaps that you are not happy with what I have to say. That is fine. I may be incorrect and absolutely I ask you to challenge me. But often, I have found that when a client is uncomfortable in a session, that is when he / she begins making the changes that lead to the results that he/she was initially seeking. It has just happened too often for it to be a coincidence.

The other aspect that is absolutely critical for the success of this program is that you are entirely honest with me and with yourself about how you feel and what you want. Sometimes what we want isn't comfortable to hear out loud, but we must face the truth. A portion of therapy may consist of reconciling between how we think we should feel and what we should want and what we really do feel and want. But, I ask you to be entirely honest and discover the true you. There is no judgment, no expectation and no predestined outcome in this process - only discovery of the truth and better, more successful outcomes.

TABLE OF CONTENTS

Session #1: 1
    The Rules 3

Sessions #2-3: 19
    Dating Roadblocks 21

Sessions #4-5: 35
    You 37

Sessions #6-7: 45
    Your Potential Partner 47

Session #8: 59
    The Search 61

Session #9: 73
    Dating Pathologies 75

Session #10-11: 87
    Your Marketing Plan 89

Sessions #1-12: 97
    Goals and Manifestations 99
    – Tracking your Results

Sessions #1-12: 103
    Timeline 105

SESSION # 1

THE RULES

. . . . for These Sessions to achieve the greatest amount of success.

RULE # 1. ONE THING AT A TIME.

It's not all about the "be all end all" – marriage or happiness. If you cannot be happy dating, how will you be happy married? That may or may not be an ultimate goal, but either way, one can be happily dating. Our society rushes to that end result. We are a goal-oriented society. Look at Hollywood. Someone's dating and immediately it has to be "it", "the one". Maybe it does not have to be "it" and that does not have to discount the experience. From your positive dating experiences, you can learn and see clearly when there is a possibility of a life long partner. Just because a relationship does not end up in marriage, does not mean it is a failure.

GOAL #1: STRIVE TO BE HAPPILY DATING ONLY.

What are your thoughts / subconscious rules about dating vs. marriage?
_____
_____
_____
_____

Have you ever tried to rush a relationship or been goal oriented about a relationship? When and Why?
_____
_____
_____
_____

Have you ever felt that marriage would make your relationship better?
_____
_____
_____
_____

How does marriage benefit you personally in a practical sense? Why do you want to be or do you even want to be married?

_____
_____
_____
_____

Have you predetermined an appropriate length of time to date before marriage? Why and how was that timetable chosen?

_____
_____
_____
_____

How does society & family influence your view of marriage? Can you be independent from them?

_____
_____
_____
_____
_____

  The most common reason that an individual gives for getting divorced or wanting to get a divorce is that they got married too young, too quickly or felt pressured to get married by their partner, family or society. Most people initiating the divorce say that they knew it was not right before they got married or shortly after, but that they stayed with this person because they felt so much pressure to do so. If we can be honest with ourselves and others and stand up to this pressure, we can develop the patience and strength to find someone that we will be able to have a long lasting relationship.

RULE #2 - MAKE A COMMITMENT TO YOURSELF, TO YOUR DATING LIFE, TO YOUR HAPPINESS.

Just like a relationship requires commitment, so does dating. Because dating isn't all roses (just like a relationship). Dating also has highs, lows and plateaus.

As with many goals, one night or day we say "Let me do this. I am going to take a step towards change and commit myself to dating". Maybe that is why you came here. Then the first bump in the road and it is "Forget men or forget women. I am better off without them." But for this program to work, you must be committed to seeing it through the good and bad moments. And not just good and bad dates, but also those moments in these sessions when you are asked to face some things about yourself that may not be pleasant. But this program is about results and to gain results it takes work, discomfort at times and commitment.

This isn't church *(the answer)*. This isn't the spa *(mmmm. Feels good)*. This is about you looking within and becoming the person you want to be and taking the steps you need to in order to find someone with whom you want to share yourself. We were not created to be alone. It is in our DNA to want to connect with someone. That is why, no matter how independent we are, there is a genuine longing for someone.

GOAL #2 – SET ASIDE A PERCENTAGE OF YOUR PIE (OF TIME, THOUGHT, ENERGY) FOR THIS DATING COMMITMENT.

What brought you here?

___
___
___
___

How are you in general with commitment and goals – at work, home etc?

___
___
___
___

What has been an obstacle in the past with regard to making the time and commitment to date or seek therapy or any type of self help?

___
___
___
___

THE RULES

Who do you have in your support network that will encourage you in this?

_____
_____
_____
_____

How does your pride or ego come into play when it comes to this commitment?

_____
_____
_____
_____

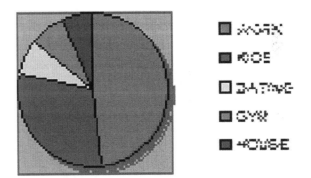

DRAW YOUR DATING COMMITMENT PIE.
(i.e. work, kids, gym, leisure, dating, house etc.)

RULE # 3 - BE HONEST WITH YOURSELF (AND WITH ME).

Therapy, communication, improvement never works and is never successful with a glossed over finish, denial or any kind of dishonesty. What is working with the opposite sex? What isn't and what is your hunch as to why. What did he/she say? How did you feel? Often we want so much for the date to be the one that we see it and the person in a better light or more compatible with us than they really are.

GOAL #3 — LOOK AT EVERYTHING HOW IT REALLY IS. DO NOT BE AFRAID OF THE TRUTH.

Explain a time when you glossed over something or were in denial

"The only thing wrong with you, Tom, is that you're almost too good to be true."

Explain a time when someone seemed so perfect and then you discovered that they weren't so perfect for you. Did they change? Or did they hide something about themselves really well? Or did your rose colored glasses fall off? It could be any one of these things.

When did they change . . .

_____
_____
_____
_____

When were they master magicians . . . .

_____
_____
_____
_____

THE RULES

When did you not see clearly . . .

How can you see them (your dates) clearly? Pointers and Red Flags

Great qualities earned too quickly:

Look at the Truth:

Look at Actions:

Talk is Cheap
one of my favorite trite sayings that is oh, so true

Internal Contradictions - Be honest with yourself and what you really want, not what you think you should want.

RULE # 4 - DON'T SUCCUMB TO OTHER PEOPLE'S RULES.

"no sex for 3 months", "sex after 3 dates or the spark isn't there", "don't date 2 people at the same time". You need to make your own rules. Have sex when *you* want to and when you do not foresee a down side, not when you think you should. And do not abstain from sex because of some rule that was designed from someone else's circumstances.

GOAL #4 – MAKE YOUR OWN DATING RULES

What are some areas that you want to make rules about (time, sex, money etc.)
_____
_____
_____
_____

What are rules that you have had in the past and why do they work or not work?
_____
_____
_____
_____

Your Rules about Time
_____
_____
_____
_____

Your Rules about Sex
_____
_____
_____
_____

Your Rules about Money
_____
_____
_____
_____

Your Rules about Commitment. When does he or she deserve or get a commitment? Why are commitments giving so quickly and freely?

___

Your Rules about Arguing

___

Your Rules about Characteristics (careful not to be too limiting here)

___

It is important to go into a relationship with some rules about what you cannot tolerate. Often couples come to me and the person they are with personifies, is and always was exactly what they knew they didn't want. "He's a cheapskate." "She's mouthy." "He screams and yells" "She isn't very sexual" They knew this before they got married, but again felt the pressure or thought that rule of theirs didn't apply because they love him or her. Love does not conquer all. Love does not conquer an engrained quality that you know you can't live with in a person and love does not guarantee that someone will change for you.

RULE # 5 - ATTRACT THE MOST OPTIONS AND THE BEST OPTIONS YOU CAN.

He or she is not going to come knocking at your door. Or it may not be the he or she you really want. It is a numbers game like anything else. If you have 1 interested, you may just chose that 1 because of our need to be with someone. If you have 10 or 20 interested, you have more options, can be more particular and focus on having the compatible relationship that you really want.

GOAL #5 – BE THE BEST CATCH YOU CAN BE TO ATTRACT THE BEST CATCH

Are you the best you can be?

_____
_____
_____
_____

What do you want to change about yourself to optimize your options?

_____
_____
_____
_____

Are you open to realizing that what you say you want in a partner and what you really want may be different? If so, why are they different?

_____
_____
_____
_____

Are you comfortable dating more than one person at a time? Why or Why Not?

_____
_____
_____
_____

How have your numbers or options been in the past?

_____
_____
_____
_____

Have you ever marketed yourself in a dating sense? How about in another sense, such as for work?

_____
_____
_____
_____

Do you think it is a numbers game? And like with true marketing, the numbers only work when you have a good list!

_____
_____
_____
_____

Do not mistake putting yourself in a situation with multiple options with this frantic searching that can happen on the internet. Sometimes on the internet the frantic search leads to the grass always seeming greener and we can never slow down enough to let a real connection happen. The message here is not about getting the highest numbers, but finding the highest numbers in quality options and paying enough attention to give those "quality leads" a chance.

RULE # 6 - REMAIN OPEN TO THE POSSIBILITY THAT DATING AND RELATIONSHIPS IN YOUR LIFE MAY BE DIFFERENT FROM WHAT YOUR FAMILY, FRIENDS AND SOCIETY EXPECT.

Our family and friends mean well. But often they are the worst counselors, advisors and therapists. Mothers often give the worst advice when it comes to partner choices because they have their agenda, their needs and their goals in the mix. Not to mention mother's have their generation's values and often times only one partner experience! Also, often, close family and friends are so protective that they do not let you live and learn for yourself.

GOAL # 6 – STAND UP TO THOSE AROUND YOU AND EXPRESS YOURSELF ASSERTIVELY

How do you truly feel about being single and what is your current position on marriage, dating etc. Rehearse it.

_____
_____
_____
_____

Now, respond to the following comments:

_____
_____
_____
_____

"I can't believe you are not married (or remarried) yet."

_____
_____
_____
_____

"You are too picky. You'll never find anyone"

_____
_____
_____
_____

"You are not getting any younger."

_____
_____
_____
_____

"You're dating someone new again? I can't keep up."

_____
_____
_____
_____

How have your family and friends meddled or judged you in the past with your relationship status?

CHECKING POINT

You are going to have to work hard and be open to change. It is easy to come here to these dating coaching sessions (fun even, very self indulgent). But you won't be successful if you don't apply what you learn and change is hard. It takes a conscious effort the older we become. Be open!

How have you changed so far in terms of each of the Program's Goals

Goal #1: Strive to be happily dating only	
Goal #2 – Set aside a percentage of your pie (of time, thought energy) for this dating commitment.	
Goal #3 – Look at everything how it really is. Do not be afraid of the truth.	
Goal #4 – Make your own dating rules	
Goal #5 – Be the best catch you can be to attract the best catch	
Goal # 6 – Stand up to those around you and express yourself assertively	

SESSIONS # 2 & 3

DATING ROADBLOCKS / OBSTACLES

Excuses / Excuses
　　What are your excuses for not dating or going on a date?
　　Immediately deciding he isn't good enough or she has an unbearable quality. (i.e. I would never date a cop; I would never date a woman with kids; I would never date someone only 5' 8" etc.)

OR

Immediately having a conflict with time, money, kids, work etc.

List your Excuses:

1.
2.
3.
4.
5.

Accept that this is an Investment
Are you willing to invest time into this to gain your result?
If you are here, I would say the answer is yes. Be prepared for . . .

10 BAD DATES FOR EVERY GOOD DATE

Take SOMETHING positive away from the bad dates, instead of getting discouraged

- Learned about a new restaurant
- Learned a new red flag
- Learned about someone interesting even though there was no attraction
- Learned something about myself
- Good practice
- Tried out a new outfit

As with anything in our life that we want to change or improve, we have to do things that we don't WANT to do – PERIOD.

There are 3 primary obstacles to dating and being happy dating:

RESISTANCE

Your mind says no so fast, it doesn't have a chance to process what could possibly be positive. And this is because

A. THE PAST

Draw a Relationship Timeline (Who were they and what did they represent)

Past							Present

DATING ROADBLOCKS / OBSTACLES

LIST PROS AND CONS OF EACH MAJOR RELATIONSHIP

Relationship	Pros	Cons
#1		
#2		
#3		

Similarities and Conclusions:

☐ REALITY CHECK
What is your past pain from dating and relationships? Summarized in a paragraph.

Once again, just as in The Rules, be honest with yourself. Men often say "she left me because I didn't make enough money" Then, down the road she marries a guy that doesn't have very much money. It is easier to say, she was superficial and wanted money instead of admitting a failure. It is easier to make it about something that you already know, such as 'I don't make that much money'. Just look at it from all sides honestly and question/challenge your first response to why things did not work out.

"DOES THIS MEAN WE'RE THROUGH?"

Questions to Ponder regarding this information:

How can you put that pain in a place where it is helpful in terms of wisdom, caution and smart decisions, but not harmful in terms of barriers, projection and baggage?

___
___
___
___

What have you learned from the past and how can it help you?

___
___
___
___

What do you tend to project from the past on new relationships?

___
___
___
___

DATING ROADBLOCKS / OBSTACLES

Negative Characteristics that I continue to attract or be attracted to

Users – I allow myself to be used. I feel that is all I have to offer

Philanderers – I blind myself and hang on to something promising that they said

Unemployed – I allow myself to get involved with someone that is not my "equal" in stability, finances or employment. Why?

Gold digger – I feel all I have to offer is money, so that is what I put out there first and I believe what they tell me about how they feel about me and that I am their sexual preference.

You may have good reason to project negative images from the past on to a new relationship because possibly you pick the same person with the same problem. This can be because that is what you are attracted to or it is what you attract.

How can I break this cycle? What might I have to give up?

_____
_____
_____
_____

What thoughts do I need to change?

_____
_____
_____
_____

Am I truly available? Do I pick those that are unavailable?

_____
_____
_____
_____

What do I honestly want?

_____
_____
_____
_____

THE DATING COACH WORKBOOK

<u>Your Issues from Past Relationships Carried Forward</u>

Relationship Cycle EXAMPLE

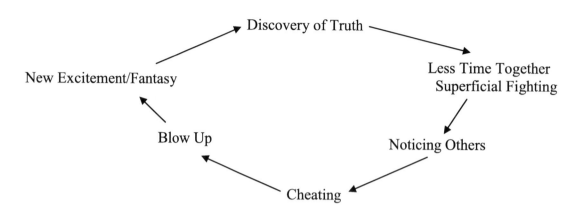

This progression makes it less hard to break up, when we are really angry or have found someone else. Instead, in order to save pain, the couple should break up in the Discovery of Truth stage.

DRAW YOUR RELATIONSHIP CYCLE

B. LACK OF SELF- CONFIDENCE OR LACK OF TAKING RESPONSIBILITY

List your own Contributions and Detriments to Relationships. What do you have to offer? What is a problem for your partners? What do they complain about with you?

_____
_____
_____
_____

DATING ROADBLOCKS / OBSTACLES

Do you believe there is someone for everyone or do you tell yourself "no one will want you?"

_____
_____
_____
_____

Re-parenting yourself through positive self talk.

_____
_____
_____
_____

Making yourself the best you can be (in the You section of this workbook) to gain new self-confidence.

_____
_____
_____
_____

C. COMFORT ZONE

It is necessary to get out of your comfort zone. Friday nights with the TV and your cat and all of the good that represents to you is going to have to be broken.

What is comfortable in your current life that you know will change when dating or in a relationship?

_____
_____
_____
_____

Is the trade off of comfort worth not having a relationship?

_____
_____
_____
_____

DATING ROADBLOCKS / OBSTACLES

REJECTION/FEAR

Many of us do not resist, we are open all the time to dating and relationships, but our issues with rejection and our fears keep us from having successful dating and relationships.

A. FEAR OF BEING ALONE LEADS TO RUSHING INTO RELATIONSHIPS

Do you go to events without a date — weddings, reunions?

_____
_____
_____
_____

Do you go to activities alone — movies, golf?

_____
_____
_____
_____

What would happen if you ended up alone?

_____
_____
_____
_____

What catastrophic thoughts do you harbor around being alone or not having someone in your life? Or growing old alone?

_____
_____
_____
_____

What rules do we have about committing and dating exclusively when we don't really know the person well enough to know if they have what we need/want?

_____
_____
_____
_____

Can you date several at a time or remain single until someone is worth investing in?

_____
_____
_____
_____

What is the difference between jealousy and suspicion?

_____
_____
_____
_____

Rushing into the wrong relationships instead of waiting for the right fit and not being unable to breakup once attached, though the issues are obvious, is probably the #1 reason my clients site for desiring a divorce.

B. FEAR OF REJECTION AND CRITICISM DURING THE DATE.

What does your mind tell you during the date when you know he/she is not interested?

These thoughts can be reframed. Here's how . . .

Put yourself in **The Drivers Seat** during the date. And then it isn't rejection, just not a fit.

Observe and Decide. No Quick Conclusions

Observe: treats others; intelligence, sense of humor etc.

Decide: (I want a second date. Not I want to marry him/her) Or maybe just decide I want a physical relationship, but don't expect more. On the first date, just decide if you want a second date – that's all

List your self-talk before the date.

_____
_____
_____
_____

List your self-talk during the date.

_____
_____
_____
_____

Role Play / Scenarios

He says "You look beautiful", I think, "
She says, "Where do your parents live", I think "
She says, "Do you want kids?", I think "
He says, "You look heavier than your picture", I think "

EXPECTATIONS

It is interesting how our expectations are so few initially when we meet someone. We just want a certain look or a way that they carry themselves. And then as we enter the relationship our list of expectations grows longer and longer and of course they cannot live up to them. They were not interviewed for this list!

Are your expectations for a partner realistic?

WHAT YOU WANT IN A PARTNER	WHAT YOU OFFER TO A PARTNER
1.	1.
2.	2.
3.	3.
4.	4.
5.	5.

Is it an even trade? Equality?

☐   REALITY CHECK

Are you willing to accept what realistically you can "get"? And what is available?

KNOW WHAT YOU OFFER...

*guy that buys girl: *don't be surprised when she isn't madly in love*

*woman that refers to beauty that isn't there: *capitalize elsewhere*

Let's face it as we get older, the options are less. The committed, positive, successful people have most likely had successful marriages. We have our warts too and we need to honestly look at them and see what we are able to attract WITHOUT ulterior motives.

DATING ROADBLOCKS / OBSTACLES

Ulterior motives work for awhile (gold diggers, users etc.) and we get someone outside of our league, but it almost always backfires and there is infidelity and pain in the end. Ultimately the objective was to take from the other and not to love. A deep connection and honesty is not attained and sooner or later someone wants something else.

CHECKING POINT

What did you change or learn about each of these Obstacles

Resistance	
Rejection/Fear	
Expectations	

What about Self-Sabotage?

Do you
not Resist
not worry about Rejection/Fear while dating
have reasonable Expectations
find a Great Match
and then ruin it?

Probably comes back to Rejection/Fear. Revisit this.

SESSIONS 4 & 5

YOU

1. APPEARANCE (THIS IS GOING TO BE BRUTALLY HONEST)

A.   Keep as many options open.

B.   Remove any obstacles (unkempt or odd teeth, hair, nails etc.)

C.   First Impressions. What first impression do you make?
        1.
        2.
        3.
        4.

D.   Superficiality is reality initially.

2. YOUR VIEW OF SELF (PHYSICALLY AND OTHERWISE)

A.   Celebrity that you look like

B.   Scale of 1 to 10

C.   Like about your face / body

D.   Dislike about your face / body

E.   Cosmetic Work – past and future considerations

F.   Your personality type – the impression that you make.

G.   Do you like your first impression? Pros and Cons of it.

PROS	CONS

☐   REALITY CHECK

3. YOUR PROFILE / FIRST IMPRESSION

A. Review profile for Internet Dating

B. What are 3 key points that are your strengths that you want someone to know about you right away?

   1.
   2.
   3.

C. What is your baggage? What might negatively impact your first impression? How can you keep it from getting in the way?

4. YOUR MINDSET DURING A DATE

A. Thoughts that run through your mind. Write down 5:

1.

2.

3.

4.

5.

B. Are these thoughts oriented towards acceptance of you?

If yes, **Change** *the orientation.*
It is about the search **not** *about his / her acceptance*

C. In your head during the date – Observe and Decide:

"Do I like him? Am I enjoying our conversation? Is this a nice time?"

NOT

"Does he like me? Do I look o.k.? He doesn't seem into me"

5. YOUR MINDSET IN DAILY ENCOUNTERS

A. Quick to write an individual off - a defense mechanism

B. Openness when out and about. Describe your day of errands, tasks etc.

C. Too eager – Reactive Attachment

D. Making excuses for yourself or the potential partner

6. HAPPINESS AND FULFILLMENT ALONE FIRST. VISUALIZE. GUIDED IMAGERY

Describe a happy moment where external forces were not responsible for your happiness, but it was within you. If you have never had this, describe how it would feel if you did.

"Happiness is when what you think, what you say, and what you do are in harmony."

Mahatma Gandhi

7. BECOME WHAT YOU SEEK.

Who do I need to become to attract what I want and have the greatest range of choice? Write about yourself as if you are character in a book.

_____
_____
_____
_____
_____
_____
_____
_____
_____

Who do I want as a partner? Write about your potential partner as if he/she were a character in a book.

_____
_____
_____
_____
_____
_____
_____
_____
_____

☐ REALITY CHECK

8. YOUR MENTAL HEALTH

We all have some part of one of these to cope.
What do you have and to what degree?
There is cause for concern when one of the issues below interferes with social and occupational functioning OR Dating . . . .

DEPRESSION

Depressed mood (variable diagnosis depending on length and severity of mood)
Loss of interest, pleasure and/or energy
Change in sleeping and eating habits
Loss of self esteem, feeling of worthlessness
Diminished ability to think or concentrate, indecisiveness
Recurrent thoughts of death
    Manic episodes including inflated self-esteem, extremely talkative, flight of ideas, excessive involvement in pleasurable activity that result in painful consequences

ANXIETY/FEAR

Difficult to control worry
Restlessness or on edge
Easily fatigued
Difficulty concentrating
Irritability
Muscle tension and difficulty sleeping
Various anxieties can be related to specific phobias or traumas

ADDICTION

Substance tolerance
Withdrawal symptoms
Persistent desire and unsuccessful effort to control
Inhibits social and occupational functioning
Substantial or extra effort required to obtain substance
Legal problems related to substance use
Physically hazardous results from substance use
Interpersonal problems related to substance use

    If there is Mental Illness that needs to be addressed, see Dating Pathologies Section.

CHECKING POINT

What did you change or learn about your:

Appearance	
First Impression	
Mindset about Town	
Mindset on a Date	
Your Personal Best	
Your Mental Health	

SESSIONS 6 & 7

YOUR POTENTIAL PARTNER

What Each Sex Wants **(generally speaking)** (Accept It. Can't Change what is Genetically Programmed)

MEN	WOMEN

WHAT ABOUT SAME SEX RELATIONSHIPS?

There are some advantages in terms of the Mars/Venus gender differences when it comes to same sex relationships. There is some commonality. Two gay men happily in a relationship often can talk to each other about the good looking guy at the bar and not be upset or jealous. They are both understanding of the visual aspect of who they are. Two lesbian women can communicate at length and explore feelings without having to pry information out of their partner, due to the general need for women to talk and explore feelings.

BUT, there is still plenty of pain and wrong decisions and poor choices in same sex relationships. All of the factors that we are exploring in this workbook including becoming our personal best, having patience for the best relationship for us, understanding our past and our own mental health are not necessarily easier to attain just because there is not the Opposite Sex obstacle.

> However, I will tell you honestly, as a heterosexual woman, often I have secretly thought:
> *"How much easier it would be to be a lesbian! She would understand me!"*

USERS

The Age Gap — 20+ years. Can it work?

There are always exceptions, but usually . . . .

Men date much younger women because they are easier to impress and as men are visual, youth looks better. At some point, superficiality has a consequence.

Women date much older men because they are looking for financial security and are helpless to take care of themselves. Sooner or later they will seek a true attraction.

Relationship Examples (list 3 celebrity or personally known relationship examples with an age span of more than 20 years and describe the dynamic)

1.

2.

3.

The Cougar Syndrome. What is the exchange here? What is the need met and the most likely outcome?
_____
_____
_____
_____

At first it feels really good to buy youth, but
_____
_____
_____
_____

Eventually, it is not going to be fulfilling to only be desired for your money
_____
_____
_____
_____

Eventually, it is not going to be fulfilling to be only desired for appearance

_____
_____
_____
_____

Often, the used party puts their money out there to get the user and then is so surprised and betrayed when eventually it is discovered that all that the user wanted was their money. He/she expects to be genuinely loved, when that was never really part of the equation. Money was the bait all along. It never changed. It does not change to genuine love – the currency remained the same.

FINANCIAL USERS

Reality is that there are only three ways to achieve financial gain or security *(which is in many ways the backbone of our existence and our culture here in America)*.

They are:

INHERITANCE
EARNING POWER
MARRIAGE

For many people, inheritance and earning power are not an option, **thus marriage is the ONLY means available to financial security**.

For many victims of financial users, it is accepted that the particular party is interested in their money and the exchange of sweetness, attractiveness etc. is a welcome trade. And, these unions can work. They can work if the one that is in need of the financial aid is a *dependent personality* and agrees to do what is needed completely to *support their partner*. If the motive by the financial dependent is selfish and designed solely to seek one's own security, then the relationship often will not work. But if the motive is to give and support another, it can work.

On the other hand, while the financial user feels that the receipt of financial security is more important than a genuine attraction, over time, the financial user does desire to feel generally attracted to their partner and to pursue that attraction. The victim then is shocked and hurt by this revelation of their partner flirting or even committing infidelity, as he/she has given so much to the relationship. However, he/she should not be surprised.

What is the difference between being a financial user and seeking someone that is financially stable?

_____
_____
_____
_____

THERE IS A BIG DIFFERENCE:

A financial user's #1 priority is to find someone that has money so that he or she will benefit directly. Other characteristics of the individual that the user is pursuing are not important if this objective is met. The financial user is plotting an act of financial gain, the way someone would go about trying to close a sales deal.

On the other hand, a person that is seeking a potential partner that is financial stable is using this criteria as just ONE of the criteria that he or she seeks in a partner, not the sole objective. And, the necessity of this criteria is in order for the individual to respect the potential partner and for the individual feel on equal or similar financial footing with the potential partner. It is a criteria that the individual feels will make a good partnership and will help to build trust for decision making and compatibility for lifestyle choices. And the partner seeking financial stability is willing to give of themselves and even sacrifice their desires in order to help their partner achieve this financial security.

Write your position on your finances and the financial status of your potential partner. Also write your placement of financial status in your search. Do not confuse financial status with responsibility and career goals.

☐ REALITY CHECK

CO-DEPENDENT AND DEPENDENCY DISORDERS

The Dependent personality is another danger in the dating world.

> "The essential feature of Dependent Personality Disorder is a pervasive and excessive need to be taken care of that leads to submissive and clinging behavior and fears of separation. This pattern begins by early adulthood and is present in a variety of contexts. The dependent and submissive behaviors are designed to elicit caregiving and arise from a self-perception of being unable to function adequately without the help of others."

The dependent personality can be very appealing at first. They satisfy one's need to be needed and to feel strong, smart, efficient and good about themselves. The desire to do everything together and to be very close and connected is exciting and the sexual intimacy is usually very close because the dependent personality needs this bond so strongly. One also feels that they can trust the dependent person. They are available and attentive and at one's beck and call. They can be accounted for.

However, over time the partner's lack of efficiency and ability to make their own decisions can prove trying and frustrating particularly if there are household and childcare duties or the need to have assistance with the household income. Over time, the individual feels that they have to do everything and they act once again surprised at this outcome when in fact they walked right into with their eyes wide open. It feels great at first to be so needed, but eventually it is simply exhausting.

Write your position on your need to be dependent or your feeling when you have a dependent partner.

IMMEDIATE RED FLAGS FOR MEN WHEN DATING A WOMAN

1. Needy, Insecure, Clingy, Desperate

Young men often want a needy, insecure and clingy woman to make them feel more powerful. But the more seasoned dater or older man knows that this leads to a woman that will not allow any independence, not bring excitement and interest to the relationship and due to her own insecurity may become excessively jealous. In particular if a woman has never been married or had children, it is very important to not give off desperation immediately. Reveal yourself over time.

2. Bitchy & Bossy

Young men will put up with bitchy for the right look. Older men have learned that bitchy means, you are always in trouble, nothing can make her happy, it is impossible to have fun or relax. So in time looks fade even faster with a bitchy attitude.

3. Stalking and Unstable behavior

An immediate "no go" for men and often will shut the door to a 2nd date no matter how interested or attracted, is if they get that Fatal Attraction vibe. Women: let the relationship happen naturally. There is no need on a first, second or third date to research and investigate myriads of information about him. You don't even know if you like him yet or like being around him, so it doesn't matter what his finances are, when he got divorced or what his kids are like. Let him reveal himself to you. Develop an instinct for truth and trust it. Women who stalk men or find out about their personal life via children's Facebook pages or public files and Google searches ruin any chance of a natural wonderful romance. It sets a foundation of distrust. Of course this applies to men as well, but is more common in women who want to rush to the end result of dating.

"THE ONLY WAY I HAD TO GET YOUR ATTENTION WAS TO SEND YOU THAT COMPUTER VIRUS."

Women: Are any of these Red Flags – you?

YOUR POTENTIAL PARTNER

IMMEDIATE RED FLAGS FOR WOMEN WHEN DATING A MAN

1.   Financial instability

Women still feel loved if a man is able to make their life easier and take care of them in some way. Women feel loved when a man pays for dinner or buys a gift. Even the most independent and successful women usually do not want to be the financial leader and often complain once they have entered a relationship with someone who is their financial inferior.

If financial hardship has ensued, it will be imperative for the woman to see that this man will rebuild himself and take action to turn around past events.

2.   Self centered braggarts

Self confidence is good. Self importance is not. Women are immediately turned off if a man never asks about her on a date or brags about himself, his money, job and worst of all the women in his past (my last girlfriend was so beautiful . . .)

3.   Noticing other women

Yes, you are visual. Yes, a beautiful women in front of you is going to register in several places in your mind and body. But, when you are on a date, you have chosen to focus on one woman for that period of time and the others need to disappear. It may not be natural, but it is something to learn to control. Head turning, will turn her off period. You have a choice: you can keep looking at all of them or have one of them, one you really want, for yourself.

"But enough about me, let's talk about my job."

Men: Are any of these Red Flags – you?

LOVE LANGUAGES

Time – spending quality time together and enjoying activities
Acts of Service – doing things for one another (clean garage, prepare taxes)
Physical Affection – touch, hugs, affection, sex
Words of Encouragement – compliments and building up endeavors of the other
Gifts – physical gifts on holidays and surprises

Prioritize the Love Languages for yourself and perhaps for your current or past dating relationship

MYSELF	MY LAST PARTNER

THE 6 NEEDS

Certainty – the need for security and knowing what you can count on
Variety – the need for spontaneity and the unexpected
Love/Connection – the need to feel loved and understood
Growth – the need to improve as a person
Contribution – the need to give back to others and society
Significance – the need to be important

Prioritize the 6 Needs for yourself and perhaps for your current or past dating relationship

MYSELF	MY LAST PARTNER

YOUR POTENTIAL PARTNER

CHECKING POINT

What did you change or learn about your Potential Partner

Protecting yourself against Users	
Red Flags	
The love you need and want	
What you can accept	

SESSION 8

THE SEARCH

A. **Your Criteria**: changing up the criteria for various results and various choices. Try a new criteria. Try a new approach. We must try something new to get different results.

Describe below your current criteria for a potential date

_____
_____
_____
_____

Describe below your current criteria for a potential partner/relationship

_____
_____
_____
_____

Do you meet your own criteria?

_____
_____
_____
_____

What would someone seeking you list on his/her criteria?

_____
_____
_____
_____

Describe the profile of the person who seeks your attributes. Does this meet your criteria?

_____
_____
_____
_____

Is your criteria realistic?

_____
_____
_____
_____

What adjustments are you willing to make?

_____
_____
_____
_____

THE SEARCH

B. **Your Availability**: Can you be a partner? Do you really want to take on the responsibility of a relationship or dating? Are you making it a priority?

Are you truly, literally and legally single?

_____
_____
_____
_____

What ties do you have to your ex-spouse or relationship?

_____
_____
_____
_____

What ties do you have to your family that may encroach on your availability?

_____
_____
_____
_____

What is your availability due to your kids or job?

_____
_____
_____
_____

Break down your week. With 100 available hours

_____

Work	
Kids	
Exercise	
Hobbies	

Relaxing	
Dating/Relationship	

Emotional availability. What keeps you from giving to another and can it be changed?

Past partners availability. Describe past issues with your partners availability.

Married / Relationship low priority due to work, kids or lack of interest

Set expectations for you and your potential partner's availability

C. **Probability** – How well does your criteria meet your availability and how well do your attributes meet your potential partners criteria?

Reasonable Criteria + Good Availability = Positive Probability

_____
_____
_____
_____

D. **Where to meet Potential Partners?** *What has worked and hasn't for you?*

1. Bars
2. Friends
3. Activities – gym, cycling, golf, church
4. Daily Routine
5. Singles Groups
6. Internet

PROS AND CONS OF INTERNET

PROS	CONS
Good Practice	Misleading
Learn some information before attraction begins	Fantasy Building
Quick beginning	Not as Natural
Several choices	Potential partners also are juggling many potential partners
	Time Consuming

E. Pheromones and Sexuality

pher·o·mone (fĕr'ə-mōn')

n.

A chemical secreted by an animal, especially an insect, that influences the behavior or development of others of the same species, often functioning as an attractant of the opposite sex.

Give off the Vibe!
What your mind is thinking, your body language will show.
_____
_____
_____
_____

What is your mind thinking when you see a potential partner?
_____
_____
_____
_____

How does this show in your body language.
_____
_____
_____
_____

Are you open to meeting someone anywhere or only in certain circumstances? Always be ready for those pheromones.
_____
_____
_____
_____

THE SEARCH

The two sides to Pheromones
1. They are so important. We need this physical chemistry for an ultimately great relationship. So, don't underestimate them, because they cannot be controlled. Often we WANT a relationship with someone because of so many wonderful qualities, but the pheromones just don't exist.
2. They aren't everything. You may feel the pheromones and then project a real relationship onto something that is just pheromones and that wears out too.

One of the major problems existing in the dating world is an individual's ability to see another person's intentions and to see clearly the extent of the potential partner's interest. Many, many people of both sexes get too attached too quickly and convince themselves that the potential partner feels more than he/she does. In their hope for what they want, they see something that is not there in order to avoid any rejection. Conversely, some people don't display their sexual energy enough so as not to make the connection about sex and don't attract as many potential partners because the pheromones are being stifled.

What is your Sexual Partner Barometer? (3 scenarios — what do you do?)

_____
_____
_____
_____

1. John showed up for our date 10 minutes late, very apologetic. He said he was happy to meet me, but did not make any comment on my appearance and I had spent about 2 hours getting ready. Throughout the date he seemed a bit occupied with the time because he had to pick up his kids at 9pm. During the date he talked a lot about his work and the kids. We had a nice conversation. He said that he enjoyed talking and kissed me on the cheek good-bye. John didn't call for a week, so I text'd him after a week and asked how he was doing. He responded by sending a long text with many details of his week. Is John interested? If John asks you on a second date, do you go?

_____
_____
_____

2. Maria showed up at the bar and was extremely hot. High boots, long hair, great figure. She wasn't much for conversation and teased me a lot about just how much I would do for her, even though we had just met - and wasn't I happily surprised. I was. We were meeting for drinks and she suggested that we go to dinner at the new Capital Grille restaurant. We had a nice time. We went back to my place and had sex. I couldn't believe it. She text'd me the next morning about how great I was in bed. She had an incredible body. I cannot believe it was so easy to find someone so great. What should be the next steps? Determine if this is a potential relationship

_____
_____
_____
_____

3. Frank and I were set up by mutual friends. He works with one of my best friend's husbands. He is a great guy, just like they said. He is polite. He is smart. He always asks how I am doing. He is punctual and he is tall. I don't find myself thinking about him until he calls though or anticipating when he will call. I know he is a committed type of guy that wants a relationship, which is what I want and there are so many jerks. I want to give him a chance, but I really have no desire to sleep with him any time soon. What should the game plan be here?

___

Actions not just words — Talk is cheap.

Clinging or reading into words said is quite common when we are very attracted to another. But when we are constantly giving them the benefit of the doubt or making excuses for them, then they either are not as interested in us as we are them or they don't know how to communicate or express that interest or show love and that will keep us frustrated through the relationship.

When have you pursued someone that did not give you enough reciprocal attention?

F.   what you put out there, you will get back

Shallow begats Shallow.
Give booty call, gets booty call.

___

What do you put out there?

___

What do you get back?

___

THE SEARCH

Can you be happy alone?

_____
_____
_____
_____

The single most significant reason, this therapist believes for the dismal failure of relationships and marriages today is that we have no patience!! We are so desperate to not be alone that we think someone is someone they are not; we make a relationship greater than it is; we rush into a relationship with clearly the wrong person or before the person deserves it or us and we are unable to break up when we know we should. Subsequently, we try to change our partner. People do not change who they are, only how they communicate or behave (if they really want to change those things)

It is imperative to have some peace and happiness alone and envision and accept it, while we wait to meet someone that possesses our criteria.

Describe your vision of being alone (in hopes of a great connection later)

_____
_____
_____
_____

When have you committed yourself to someone before they deserve it?

_____
_____
_____
_____

A Note to Age 50+ Women

1. *I'm not that kind of girl.* Be that kind of girl. The biggest fear of 50+ men are that their women are post menopausal without a sex drive. Regardless of your standard as to when to actually do the deed in terms of the dating cycle, communicate clearly that you are interested in it!
And if you are not interested in it, get interested. Let your mind and body open up to sexual thoughts and feelings. It has been proven again and again regardless of age or even attractive qualities – sexual women / women that exude an interest in sex just seem to find partners easier.

2. *Princess Principals.* It works when you are 15, 20, 30 and maybe even early 40's. It really does. It tells the man that you are worthy of being treated like Princess. But now on the down cycle of life, when these men have been taken to the cleaners, manipulated by women (not someone like you of course) they may not roll out the red carpet right away. They need some time to know they can trust you. They also most likely do not fall in love at first sight anymore. So when they text you instead of calling you for a date, or do not open your car door – just take some time to get to know them before writing them off. Overtime, a good guy will see this one is worth special treatment.

3. *Desperado.* It may seem like he is the last available man on earth, but keep telling yourself he isn't! Coming across too eager or too desperate, at any age is still a big turn off.

4. *TRUST* – Trust takes time. When we trust someone before they have earned it (not enough time to know) or mistrust someone because of our past, this we mistreat the notion of Trust. Trust takes time. Don't give it away until it is earned. Don't hold it back because it is not yet earned. Just wait – patience.

THE SEARCH

CHECKING POINT

What have you learned about your Search

Your Criteria	
Your Availability	
Your Probability	
Best Places for you to Meet Someone	
Your Pheromones / Sexuality	
Your Patience	

SESSION 9

DATING PATHOLOGIES

This section is devoted to the pathological behaviors that can take place in men and women during the dating process. It is interesting that people who are very highly functional and successful in their business, parenting and friendship relationships can partake in very unhealthy behaviors when dating. And by pathological, it is not implied that there is danger, though it is possible, but instead the approach to dating when pathological is not healthy and can have a negative outcome for your dating success.

Below are the various pathologies that occur during the dating relationship. You may have displayed one or more of these behaviors or you may have experienced dating someone who displayed such a behavior.

FANTASY AND DELUSION

In particular, in the environment of cyber space relationships, "things" are not always as they appear. Potential partners meet over the internet and in the hopes of finding the perfect match, may project what they want on to a person who seems to fit a portion of their desire. It is easy to read into words said or attributes conveyed, but we must remember, we do not know them and are not testing the relationship in a real, live way. We are not around this person every day, so we have no way of knowing if the claimed attributes are true, even if the individual believes them to be true.

Remember these points:

A. You cannot know someone that you have not met.
B. You need to spend time in a variety of situations over a significant amount of time before you know how someone will behave and who they are.
C. If someone seems to good to be true or too perfect, he/she probably is.
D. Beware of users and ulterior motives.
E. If someone falls for you instantly, it is not you that they are falling for, because they do not know you. They are falling for the idea of you or what they hope you will be. And it will come crashing down in some way. Even if it ultimately works out, you may not be who they thought you were at the beginning.

Attachment Disorders and Borderline Personalities

When individuals do not attach properly to their care givers in childhood, when they are not made to feel secure and loved, then they develop attachment issues. Often these children, and later adults, attach too quickly to those that have not earned their love and trust and then eventually are not able to trust or love someone who has earned it.

These pathologies in the greatest form can manifest themselves into someone that has Borderline Personality Disorder. The traits for this disorder are:

(1) Frantic efforts to avoid real or imagined abandonment
(2) A pattern of unstable and intense interpersonal relationships characterized by alternating between extremes of idealization and devaluation
(3) Identity disturbance: unstable self image
(4) Impulsivity, self-damaging (eating, sex, spending, substance abuse)
(5) Suicidal or self mutilating behavior
(6) Affective instability due to marked reactivity of mood
(7) Chronic feelings of emptiness
(8) Inappropriate intense anger and difficulty controlling anger
(9) Transient, stress related paranoid ideation

For a Personality Disorder to clinically be validated, 5 or more of the above criteria occurs along with 2 of the following General diagnostic criteria must be present:

(1) Cognition (unrealistic ways of perceiving and interpreting self and others)
(2) Affectivity (range, intensity, appropriateness of response)
(3) Interpersonal functioning
(4) Impulse Control

However, even if you or someone you dated does NOT have Borderline Personality disorder, a person can demonstrate some of the traits associated due to a lack of proper attachment in childhood. And therefore, there is room for growth and change through mindfulness and reality therapy.

Actions that may take place that indicate that a particular person may have some Borderline Personality Traits are:

A. Stalking, following, checking up to often
B. Researching information thoroughly on the internet about a person instead of allowing the person to share about themselves
C. Using extreme descriptions about someone that he/she has just met such as "we love each other because", "he is always sincere", "she will never hurt me or cheat on me"
D. Not listening to signals from the other party, which indicate they have someone else or want to break up. Determined to convince another to stay with him/her.
E. Continually asking for reassurance and communicating desperation for the relationship.
F. Getting very angry over something that is not your place to be angry over. (i.e. the person you are seeing is dating someone else even though he/she never indicated that there was a commitment) or (the person you are seeing forgot your birthday even though you just met and they didn't remember you mentioning the exact date)

In the dating relationship, one person does not own another. It is a time to observe and decide what you like and do not like about this person and if you are going to desire a commitment with this person. **This is not the time to test trust or abandonment because the promise/commitment has not been made.**

Discuss/Express your experience with Fantasy and Delusion / Inappropriate Attachment:

CONTROLLING BEHAVIOR / POTENTIAL DOMESTIC VIOLENCE

Once again, timing and commitment must be weighed proportionately to the appropriateness or inappropriateness of the intensity.

If someone finds out after a 15 year marriage and 3 children that their wife, whom they have supported financially for 15 years and who they feel they loved and cherished is sleeping with their best friend, they are going to become temporarily insane and may possibly partake in some unhealthy behaviors. *(think Richard Gere in Unfaithful)*. It would be best if they sought help before their emotions become so out of control that they act unwittingly, but it is understandable. This is the definition of the crime of passion, the heat of the moment etc. and is standard human nature.

However, in a dating environment, these behaviors of control, violence, explosive intermittent anger are not appropriate ever. And often those individuals who create domestic violence in their later committed homes, did in fact show domestic violence traits during the dating period.

Some occurrences and feelings between the perpetrator and the victim:

Perpetrator *(Controlling Personality)*	**Victim** *(Dependent Personality)*
Calls many, many times per day	Feels loved and wanted before feeling annoyed
Distrusts any other members of opposite sex in their dating partner's life	His/Her jealousy makes them feel loved, when in fact often the perpetrator cheats and lives a double standard
Never engages in a selfless act of giving something up for him/herself in order to please the dating partner	Continually changes own plans and gives up own activities to not upset dating partner
Needs something from the relationship – financial, home stability, ownership	Gives up own comfort to please dating partner
Very low self esteem – feels attacked or injured emotionally if partner questions something said	Must be very careful about what he/she or his/her kids say or do around dating partner
Shows power and tries to gain control of chaotic inner self by violent behavior	Allows violent behavior and is unable to cut off relationship due to fear and guilt that he/she caused the violence

Anti-social, Narcissistic and Dependent Personality Disorders can be a part of the pathology in those exhibiting these behaviors. The Anti-Social and the Narcissistic Personality is the Perpetrator. The Dependent Personality is the Victim.

The primary difference between the Anti-Social and Narcissistic Personality is that the Anti-Social is more violent and destructive externally. The Narcissistic Personality does more damage emotionally. Both are extremely self centered and selfish and are unable to actually think outside of their own needs. Both also have an element of delusion of reality in their view on life and seek Dependent personalities because they must have this domination.

Please do not confuse Anti-Social Personality with someone who does not like to socialize or does not have friends. Anti-Social personality has much more of an affect on society and others than that. In fact, many of our prison inmates have anti-social personalities.

First of all, a Personality disorder is determined when the following criteria are met:

General Criteria: Exerience and behavior that deviates markedly from the expectations of the individual's culture including

1. Cognition (ways of perceiving and interpreting self, other people and events)
2. Affectivity (the range, intensive, lability and appropriateness of emotional response)
3. Interpersonal function
4. Impulse control

This criteria is then pervasive across a broad range of situations, leads to significant distress, can be traced back to adolescence or early adulthood and is not due to a physiological effects such as drug or medication abuse or a medical condition.

ANTI-SOCIAL PERSONALITY DISORDER

Specifically, The criteria for Anti-Social Personality disorder is:

There is a pervasive pattern of disregard for and violation of the rights of others occurring since age 15 years (individual is at least 18 years of age), as indicated by 3 or more of the following:

1. failure to conform to social norms with respect to lawful behaviors as indicated by repeatedly performing acts that are grounds for arrest
2. deceitfulness, as indicated by repeated lying, use of aliases or conning others for personal profit or pleasure
3. impulsivity or failure to plan ahead
4. irritability and aggressiveness, as indicated by repeated physical fights and assaults
5. reckless disregard for safety of self or others
6. consistent irresponsibility, as indicated by repeated failure to sustain consistent work behavior or honor financial obligations
7. lack of remorse, as indicated by being indifferent to or rationalizing having hurt, mistreated or stolen from another.

Are these traits familiar to anyone in your life?

_____
_____
_____
_____

Do you possess any of these traits?

_____
_____
_____
_____

NARCISSISTIC PERSONALITY DISORDER

Please do not confuse Narcissistic Personality Disorder with someone with extreme confidence. Donald Trump may be Narcissistic because he is very proud of himself and his accomplishments, but it would not appear that he has Narcissistic Personality Disorder. Those with Narcissistic Personality Disorder are not in touch with reality. So, though they have a strong sense of self-importance and may be completely self centered, they are unable to function effectively and rarely enjoy any type of worldly or financial success.

THE CRITERIA FOR NARCISSISTIC PERSONALITY DISORDER IS:

1. has grandiose sense of self-importance (exaggerates achievements and talents, expects to be recognized as superior without commensurate achievements)
2. is preoccupied with fantasies of unlimited success, power, brilliance, beauty or ideal love
3. believes that he or she is "special" and unique and can only be understood by or associate with other special or high status people or institutions
4. requires excessive admiration
5. has sense of entitlements (unreasonable expectations of especially favorable treatment or automatic compliance with his or her expectations)
6. is interpersonally exploitative, takes advantage of others to achieve his or her own ends
7. lacks empathy; is unwilling to recognize or identify with feelings of or needs of others
8. is often envious of others and believes others are envious of him or her
9. shows arrogant, haughty behaviors or attitudes

Are these traits familiar to anyone in your life?

_____
_____
_____
_____

Do you possess any of these traits?

_____
_____
_____
_____

DEPENDENT PERSONALITY DISORDER

The Dependent Personality is the ideal victim for the Anti-Social and Narcissistic Personality. This personality wants to be needed at any cost and is desperate for acceptance. So, this personality will put up with the extreme antics and abuse from the former.

THE CRITERIA FOR DEPENDENT PERSONALITY ARE AS FOLLOWS:

1. has difficulty making everyday decisions without an excessive amount of advise and reassurance from others
2. needs others to assume responsibility for most major areas of his or her life
3. has difficulty expressing disagreement with others because of fear of loss of support or approval, not including realistic fears of retribution
4. has difficulty initiating projects or doing things on his or her own because of lack of self-confidence in judgment or abilities rather than lack of motivation or energy
5. goes to excessive lengths to obtain nurturance and support from others, to the point of volunteering to do things that are unpleasant
6. feels uncomfortable or helpless when alone because of exaggerated fears of being unable to care for himself or herself
7. urgently seeks another relationship as a source of care and support when a close relationship ends
8. is unrealistically preoccupied with fears of being left to take care of himself or herself

Are these traits familiar to anyone in your life?

_____
_____
_____
_____

Do you possess any of these traits?

_____
_____
_____
_____

Domestic Violence Pattern that is often exhibited in relationships when these Personality disorders are present

DATING PATHOLOGIES

Discuss history of violence in your relationships as the perpetrator or the victim

A Word on Pathological Email and Phone "checking"

It is very common today with the various methods of social media and available communication, for a dating partner to get into the habit of invading the privacy of their dating partner and check their phone, email, blogs etc to see "what else is going on" or to find out if they can trust this partner once a commitment has been made. (the behavior is more damaging and completely unwarranted if a commitment has not even been made)

This is an unhealthy relationship behavior, always. Even when one checks the phone and email for some clue of an interlude, the "checker" is still not satisfied until he or she finds something – real or imagined.

The focus instead needs to be on the relationship. Is he paying attention to me? Are we having satisfying and frequent sexual relations? Do we feel close? Are we having fun? Are we making plans? Are we fighting too much? Does she include me? Trust and let the relationship happen naturally. The symptoms of cheating or infidelity will reveal themselves and those are what are to be addressed.

Everyone needs their privacy and no one is ever going to like *everything* their partner is thinking or saying to others. She may tell her mother something about him or he may talk to someone at work in a way she does not like. With a great relationship, each party is to protect the relationship against a potentially threatening situation, but even when that is being done – still we may have a hurt feeling or reaction to some quip or thought made by our partner to someone else. Save the negative emotion! Sometimes it is better not to be able to see everything our partner thinks.

I am not advocating turning a blind eye. Not at all. Address issues in the relationship and shoot for the best relationship always. Have a strong instinct and know your partner. But the mistrust that is evident in the checking behavior does more damage than it ever does good.

My mother and father have truly one of the best 55+ year marriages around, confirmed by all of their friends and family and most importantly by them. They have fun, are affectionate and intimate, communicate well, support one another and earnestly strive to make one another happy – it is a great marriage. When I was about 10 years old, I had a conversation with my mother that stuck with me vividly for years. I had asked her one day when she was preparing dinner, why Dad was sometimes not home until 6:30pm, when he always left work around 5:00pm and his work was not more than 30 minutes away. She responded immediately *"well, if he has another family, they don't get much of his time"*. Exactly! The relationship was going well. He adored her. Was there for her. They were close and he gave her no reason to doubt his devotion. Who knows - maybe he needed a little time alone and a scotch and soda before entering a household full of kids. **Give each other a little privacy.**

CHECKING POINT

What Pathologies have you experienced, either as the pathological or the receiver. And what have you learned from this session about domestic violence and the affect it has had on your life.

Fantasy / Delusion *(Borderline Personality Disorder)*	
Perpetrator *(Anti-Social Personality Disorder)*	
User *(Narcissistic Personality Disorder)*	
Victim *(Dependent Personality Disorder)*	
Actions you will take to avoid Dating Pathologies	
Actions you will take to resolve your Dating Pathologies	

SESSION 10

YOUR MARKETING PLAN

Lead Generation: *About Town – Always Aware, Ready and Open*

What rules do you have that are limiting your chances to meet someone?

_____
_____
_____
_____

("can't meet someone at a bar; on the internet; at work; a child's friend's parent etc")
Sometimes we have a history or have seen a relationship not work when the couple met under certain circumstances. So, we tell ourselves that we do not want to meet someone under those circumstances and by making that rigid decision we are not open to many potential relationships.

_____
_____
_____
_____

How do you look when you go to work, the gym, on errands? What changes can you make in your appearance that show that you are open to meeting someone anywhere

___
___
___
___

What is your mindset at work, the gym, son's baseball game and on errands? Are you open?

___
___
___
___

Putting out the "I like sex" vibe. It helps to attract the opposite sex. This is not suggesting forward or inappropriate sexual talk that devalues, but healthy light talk of sexual views.

Do you put out the vibe? Do you like sex? Is your vibe too obvious and asking nothing in return? Discuss. Come to a comfortable place with this.

___
___
___
___

Do you make decisions that something could fail before it has even begun? Do you see a potential obstacle and write someone off before you give him/her a chance?

("can't be with someone with 5 kids. Can't be with someone that pays alimony. Can't be with someone that is not taller than me")

___
___
___
___

WORK

___
___
___

YOUR MARKETING PLAN

Describe and explore your dating opportunities through your job – directly or indirectly. List potential people at work and list potential activities through work that could lead to meeting someone.

_____
_____
_____
_____

HOBBIES AND ACTIVITIES

_____
_____
_____
_____

Describe and explore your dating opportunities through your hobbies and activities – current and potential activities. List potential people that you are associated with through these activities and list potential activities that could lead to meeting someone.

_____
_____
_____
_____

DATING EVENTS

What dating organizations have you been involved in? What has worked and what hasn't? What are some dating organizations that you would like to become involved in? What is your goal or target for # of times per month that you will attend a dating event of some kind. Speed Dating, Meet Up groups and Local Singles groups are great options

_____
_____
_____
_____

FRIENDS

A large percentage of happy couples met through friends or friends of friends. List your friends below that may be able to introduce you to someone or invite you to an event where you could meet someone. Ask each of these friends within the next week if they have anyone they could set you up with or any activity where single people attend that they could invite you to.

_____
_____
_____
_____

Friend	Activity or Person of Interest	Date of Activity or Set Up

INTERNET

_____
_____
_____
_____

The internet is great practice for dating. Join maybe 3 sites – age appropriate and do not take it too seriously. Be honest in your profile and realistic about your expectations.

THE 4 P'S. WRITE YOUR DATING MARKETING PLAN

Product — What is your product (yourself as a partner/date). Describe your product, the benefits and the need met as you would if you were marketing a product or service.

Place — List your distribution channels. Where and how you will fill the need and find your audience.

Promotion — List the actions/steps that you will take to promote your product

Price — What are you going to ask for in exchange for your product. What are your requirements, so your needs are met as you are meeting his/her needs.

With this logical marketing approach to finding our partner, not for a minute does this program discount the need for pure pheromones, love and chemistry. This program is designed to find a great love/a partner and to absolutely attract the most options possible to find that fit. It does not replace natural desire for another.

SELF-SABOTAGE

Explore the self-sabotage that may occur of not allowing oneself to be attracted to a logical partner.

Physical Attraction: Must stay true to this. Agreed that one cannot make themselves become attracted to someone just because they seem like a good fit. The initial attraction, physical, personality, humor etc. must be there.

Availability: Sometimes we choose unavailable partners as a protection against making a commitment yourself. Do you really want a commitment or are you choosing unavailable partners to avoid it?

Dating Down: Dating less than desirable partners so that you are always in the drivers seat, making the decisions and will not be able to be hurt. This way you are in control, but you are not getting what you really want. Often you will not treat the partner very well when you have dated down.

CHECKING POINT

As with any good marketing plan, how do we measure our ROI – return on investment. How will you measure the return in each of these areas.

Number of Dates:	
Quality of Dates:	
Confidence in Self:	
Peace with Self and the Dating Process:	

SESSIONS 1 – 12

GOALS AND MANIFESTATIONS

Now comes the time for change. List 3 Goals (or more) that will change your past behavior and create a more positive result. Describe this goal clearly.

Choose 3 specific manifestations of this goal in a practical way - how will you very realistically and very practically carry out this goal. Also list 2-3 ways you will know the manifestation has been successful

Then, under each manifestation, plot the results of it every 2 months for 6 months

EXAMPLE

A. Become the Best Catch that I can be

1. My Product improves
   a) Lose 10 pounds. Gym 5 times per week (classes/social)
   b) Start side business. Extra money and join business marketing group (meet potential dating partners or friends)
   c) Think of others and help others. Karma. Improving Personality

2. Dating Confidence improves
   a) Go to one Single social event per week. And just be proud of myself socially. Doesn't matter if I meet anyone
   b) 1 date per week. Internet or going out on Friday or Saturday. Without friends – more approachable
   c) Evaluate each date in terms of my being at ease and my confidence. Nothing to do with him. Not the focus now

3. Improve my insight to what I need in a relationship
   a) Seek someone that is supportive. They won't have my energy or success maybe, but need nice / supportive now in life
   b) Explore sexual thoughts, as I am approaching menopause and don't want that to go away . . .

Chart the Manifestation Results

	2 months	4 months	6 months
Mani #1	5 pounds	10 pounds	Side business just started
Mani #2	2 social events/month	2 dates per month and 2 social events per month	1 date per week. Trying not to settle
Mani #3	Choosing nicer men for dates	Attracting the right men for me. Sexually active	Still waiting for right combo of attraction and supportive. Getting closer.

YOURS

A.

1.

   a)
   b)
   c)

2.
   a)
   b)
   c)

3.
   a)
   b)
   c)

Chart the Manifestation Results

	2 months	4 months	6 months
Mani #1			
Mani #2			
Mani #3			

B.

1.
a)
b)
c)

2.
a)
b)
c)

3.
a)
b)
c)

Chart the Manifestation Results

	2 months	4 months	6 months
Mani #1			
Mani #2			
Mani #3			

SESSIONS 1 – 12

TIMELINE

MONTH:

Sunday	Monday	Tuesday	Wednesday	Thursday	Friday	Saturday

MONTH:

Sunday	Monday	Tuesday	Wednesday	Thursday	Friday	Saturday

MONTH:

Sunday	Monday	Tuesday	Wednesday	Thursday	Friday	Saturday

MONTH:

Sunday	Monday	Tuesday	Wednesday	Thursday	Friday	Saturday

GOALS AND MANIFESTATIONS

MONTH:

Sunday	Monday	Tuesday	Wednesday	Thursday	Friday	Saturday

MONTH:

Sunday	Monday	Tuesday	Wednesday	Thursday	Friday	Saturday

REFERENCES

The Evolution of Psychotherapy "Strategic Therapy with a Couple" Cloe Mandanes, HDL, 2009

"Love Languages" Gary D. Chapman, Dec 2009

DSM IV TR, Diagnostic Statistical Manual of Mental Disorders DSM IV-TR, Fourth Edition, Text Revision, American Psychiatric Association, June 2000

Cartoonstock.com

Made in the USA
Middletown, DE
17 September 2015